Discovering God in our Everyday Lives

**There is no such thing as an ordinary day for a Christian.
With Christ, every day, every task, every situation, every relationship
brims with divine possibility. God is always at work.**

But can we see it?

The one about… is a collection of true stories about people, with names
changed, who God has been working in and through in their everyday
Monday to Saturday lives. That's not to say that all these people were sharply
aware of how God was working – often they weren't, until someone asked
them about it, or simply pointed it out. Actually, many of us are like that.
We can't see what others can see. Indeed, many of the Christians I meet don't
really think that God is doing much in their lives, and genuinely struggle to
see how they might have done anything of any great significance for him.
Often, it takes a while for people to see the beauty of what God has
been doing.

Encouragingly, one of the ways we can learn to see God's hand more quickly
is to reflect on our lives in the light of the Bible. For example, we might ask
ourselves: What connection or parallel do I see between the way God acted in
David's or Deborah's life and the way he seems to be acting in mine?

forefathers in the faith have sought to follow him, and about how, as Paul puts it, we imitate them as they imitate Christ.

Of course, our testimonies, our eyewitness accounts, of God's action in our lives are not meant to displace the great story of God's actions in time and his supreme revelation of himself through Christ, but further illuminate it.

Similarly, we listen to the stories of the ways our contemporary sisters and brothers are living out their trust in Christ and we respond in praise, or wonder, or repentance. And perhaps God uses those stories to help us see how we might express our love for Christ in our particular context – to his glory.

'Go home to your own people and tell them how much he has done for you, and how he has had mercy on you'
Mark 5:19

Furthermore, the stories of God's continuing action in his world serve to increase my wonder at Christ's sacrifice on the cross and at the power of his transformative love. They highlight how Christ's work on the cross reverberates through the centuries, crosses all boundaries of race, age, and culture, penetrates the deepest recesses of the most wounded or the most leaden heart, and radiates the smile of the Father's face turned in loving invitation to all people – come to me and live life to the full.

Read, share, discuss...

As you'll see, we've laid the stories out so you can use them in a variety of ways. You can just read them all the way through on your own. Alternatively, you could read one in a group and discuss what strikes others. You could also stop at the pause point and ask how you or others might have acted, or ponder the question at the end of the story, or use these four questions to help you:

What aspect of God's character do you see in the story?

What godly characteristic(s) does the person display?

What connection with your own life or a friend's life do you see?

What biblical story or verse or passage or truth does it remind you of?

You'll also see that there are some pages that we've left blank for you to jot down one of your own experiences with God. I hope you will.

May the Father who loves you,
The Son who sends you,
The Spirit who empowers you,
Be with you and bless you,
Wherever you are, whatever you do, whoever you're with,
To his praise and glory.

Mark Greene

'I will give thanks to you, LORD, with all my heart; I will tell of all your wonderful deeds.'

Psalm 9:1

The one about...
Victoria's secret

Victoria is an apprentice hairdresser. She's 19 and she's been in the job just over a month. It's a busy salon so there's always something to do and it's almost always got to be done quickly. She's enjoying it – the people are upbeat, friendly – but she's been feeling the pressure. Three weeks into the job, and her vicar prays for her, commissions her into the job. She's been more at peace since then. I ask her:

'So, what difference does being a Christian make to the way you wash someone's hair?'

I wonder what you might say if someone asked you that question about what you do every day. I wonder what you might say if you were a hairdresser.

Victoria didn't miss a beat:

'I pray for them as I massage in the conditioner.'

I wonder what strikes you about that 'little' story. What convictions shape Victoria's day and her actions? What biblical connections do you see?

10

Victoria's praying is an invisible gift to her clients – soothing conditioner for the soul, not just the hair. Still, behind her prayers lie a whole set of beliefs.

Victoria believes that her daily context in a hairdressing salon is important to God. And why shouldn't she? Is it not the case that 'the earth is the Lord's and everything in it' (Psalm 24:1)?

She believes that the actual work she does is important to God, that the work itself can be done in a distinctive way: the actual massaging in of the conditioner, kneading it into the scalp, learning what level of pressure is both effective and relaxing for each individual uniquely created in the image of God. No doubt Paul, the Apostle and tentmaker who wrote to slaves in Colossae and encouraged them to do 'whatever' they did as 'working for the Lord', would have been cheering her on (Colossians 3:23–24).

Victoria believes that God is alive and can move in a hairdressing salon. And why not? This is the God who intervened in a fiery furnace in Babylon to rescue Shadrach, Meshach, and Abednego (Daniel 3:8–30), the God who intervened on a lake in Galilee to still a raging storm (Mark 4:35–41), who intervened outside a tomb in Bethany to raise Lazarus from the dead (John 11:1–45).

She believes that God wants to bless her clients, and that she can be part of that. After all, is this not the God

'Whatever you do, work at it with all your heart, as working for the Lord, not for human masters, since you know that you will receive an inheritance from the Lord as a reward. It is the Lord Christ you are serving.'
Colossians 3:23–24

who sends rain to the righteous and unrighteous (Matthew 5:45), who is not willing that any should perish (2 Peter 3:9), whose essence is love (1 John 4:8), and who sends his people to love their neighbour as themselves (Matthew 22:39)?

Victoria believes in the power of prayer and in God's freedom to respond in his own way and in his own time. She doesn't need to see the results of those prayers. Indeed, this side of heaven, for the most part she probably won't. But it's still worth praying – God will be listening to her.

• • •

Is there some 'little thing'
you do in a way that consciously
involves God?

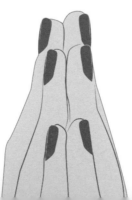

'I wash my hands in innocence, and go about your altar, LORD, proclaiming aloud your praise and telling of all your wonderful deeds.'

Psalm 26:6–7

No. 10

There are fifteen of us in this room, all men, and all from my church. Richard, whose day job is in telecoms, is leading the session. He has just asked us this question:

'What are you good at in the Lord at work?'

Yes, it's a slightly jargony way of putting it but we all knew what he meant. Still, we're English (mostly), we're men, we're from the South of England, and we're Christians. Does Richard seriously expect any of us to publicly proclaim that we're good at something, never mind good at something 'in the Lord'?

And no one does.

So Richard says, 'Why don't you write something down on a post-it note?' There are several stacks of post-it notes in front of us. It seems that he's anticipated our reticence.

So we all write something down. And then Richard says, 'Well, now you've written it down, you might as well share it.'

Clever, eh?

Mike is the first. He speaks quietly, tentatively really.

'As some of you know, I am a policeman. I'm part of the armed protection team. At No. 10.'

He had our attention at 'armed protection'.

'It's a pretty macho group of people and over the years there's been quite a lot of conflict. I've found that I am pretty good at bringing people back together.'

That's all he says.

And then he looks down at the coffee table in front of him.

Well, on that evening in that room, there's a pause – not long enough to be awkward, but definitely a pause. And then someone says, 'You've got a ministry of reconciliation.'

And a smile the width of Kansas stretches across Mike's face. It's the joy of recognition, not pride. Someone else says, 'Yes, you're a peacemaker.'

I wonder if anything strikes you about that story. How might you have responded to Mike? What biblical connections do you see?

'Blessed are the peacemakers for they will be called sons and daughters of God' (Matthew 5:9). And we all begin to see that here's a man teaching people who don't know Jesus how to forgive one another. Here's a man teaching people Jesus' way of forgiveness at No. 10 Downing Street. And that's certainly worth celebrating.

Yes, Mike had a sense that he had been doing something good but his joy was released when someone helped him see it through the lens of the Bible, helped him see that this was something that God would be pleased about, helped him see that God was working in and through him for the good of others. *God* was working through him. God was working through *him*. God!

No wonder he was so joyful.

'Blessed are the peacemakers for they will be called sons and daughters of God.'
Matthew 5:9

We grow in confidence and joy when other Christians help us see and celebrate what God is doing in and through us. And that can be as simple as getting used to asking each other questions that get us thinking: What's God been teaching you? Where have you seen God at work in your life?

That's what Richard did. You might say that he was making a rather bold assumption. After all, he was assuming that every man in that room was 'good at something in the Lord at work'. He was assuming that God had been at work in their lives and had been producing good fruit. What a wonderful assumption. And he turned out to be right. We all had something to share. But in Richard's case it wasn't really an assumption at all. Richard could ask the question not because he knew the people in the room but because he knew the God they followed. He was confident in this: God is at work in people's lives. It's what he promises, after all. He's made us new creations in Christ (2 Corinthians 5:17), he's filled us with his Spirit, and as Paul puts it: 'for it is God who works in you to will and to act in order to fulfil his good purpose' (Philippians 2:13).

And one of the great gifts we can give to one another is to help each other see it.

• • •

Is there something that you are 'good at in the Lord' in your daily life?

'Many, LORD my God,
are the wonders you have
done, the things you
planned for us. None can
compare with you;
were I to speak and tell
of your deeds, they
would be too many
to declare.'

Psalm 40:5

The one about...
the travelling Trenemans

Gary and Amahle Treneman do quite a lot of their travelling by bus. They've got to the age where it's free and anyway they don't own a car. Besides, it's always a bit of an adventure, not, I hasten to add, because life has got so dull that standing in the pouring rain waiting for the 141 is the highlight of their week but because, well, they never know quite what might happen.

I wonder, what might make travelling by bus a bit of an adventure to people who've been travelling on buses for 60 years?

What might make something you often do a bit of an adventure?

Just last week they were on the 288 coming back from the opticians. Amahle sat down next to a woman who started talking to her. She was, according to Gary, 'quite young really, only about 78'. As it happens, they got off at the same stop and Amahle said to her, 'We are Christians and before we leave home, we ask God to guide us to people. We don't stand on street corners handing out booklets but if the person initiates a conversation with us we take that as God's guidance to offer a booklet about his love.' And the 'young woman' beamed at her, took the booklet, and gave her a big hug. And Amahle asked her name and said that they'll be praying for her.

And that's why every journey is an adventure – whether they're sauntering down the road to the bus stop, or to the school gate to pick up their granddaughter, or to the shops, they pray that God will bring people to them. And often he does. And neither of them can remember anyone actually refusing the booklet. Often people start sharing their problems and challenges very quickly – which might surprise you if you hadn't met Gary and Amahle. But there's something warm about them, something calm, something that makes you feel they're more likely to listen than to interrupt, something that makes you feel they won't judge you.

I wonder what strikes you. What biblical connections do you see?

Gary and Amahle don't push it. They're not guilt-driven, they're not striving, they're not worried that they are the only people in the world that God has to reach these people and that this is the only moment in time that these people will get to hear the good news. They're trusting in God's timing, in his knowledge of whether these people are ripe to hear the kind of message that God has been shaping in Gary and Amahle's hearts these many years. They're at ease but alert to God's prompting, to his sovereign weaving in time and place, and to his love for people on whatever journey they find themselves. And there's the thing, God is leading.

Of course, God doesn't limit his ministry to their travelling. On one occasion, Amahle was itching to leave work and get home but she sensed the Holy Spirit telling her to go to the canteen. Over the years, she's learned to know the Shepherd's voice (John 10:27). So she went, bought a cup of tea and sat down. Before long, she heard someone crying some way behind her. It was a woman of about 19 or 20. She went over, introduced herself, sat down, listened, and then invited the young woman – Keira – to come round to her house the following day for a cup of tea and a chat. Extraordinarily, the young woman came. As the conversation progressed, Amahle shared the gospel and Keira became Christ's. 'It was', Gary said, 'like picking ripe fruit.' Subsequently, Keira joined the church they were part of.

'Now a man who was lame from birth was being carried to the temple gate called Beautiful, where he was put every day to beg from those going into the temple courts. When he saw Peter and John about to enter, he asked them for money. Peter looked straight at him, as did John. Then Peter said, "Look at us!" So the man gave them his attention, expecting to get something from them.

Then Peter said, "Silver or gold I do not have, but what I do have I give you. In the name of Jesus Christ of Nazareth, walk."'
Acts 3:2–6

23

Sometimes in the Bible God's leading is obvious. So, for example, an angel of the Lord tells Philip to go south onto the desert road (Acts 8:26–40). There he meets

the Ethiopian eunuch, sitting in his chariot reading Isaiah out loud. Now, as an entry point for a conversation about Christ, it doesn't get much easier. On other occasions, it's less clear but still we're invited to recognise God's leading, God's timing. Take, for example, the lame man sitting at the Gate Beautiful on Peter and John's route into the Temple (Acts 3:1–10). He was there, the text tells us, 'every day' so James and John, and Jesus too, must have walked past him many, many times, and not stopped to pray for him.

But suddenly on that day... God's leading, surely, on their journey from here to there.

Over the years, Gary and Amahle have seen God do so many amazing things on their journeys from here to there on public transport that even if someone were to give them a car, I'm not sure they'd use it that much. After all, they don't go out to catch a bus, they go out on a mission trip.

• • •

Can you think of times away from church when you've felt nudged by the Holy Spirit to do something?

'All people will fear;
they will proclaim
the works of God
and ponder what he
has done.'

Psalm 64:9

The one about...

Alan's half hour

Alan can't for the life of him see why God still has him in this organisation.

It's a chill place – this big bank – and he's been thinking about leaving for a while. He's been brought in to a team that's being led by a much younger man who's destined for great things but who right now needs an older head to steady the ship. Alan is that older head. There are 130 in the team, their profitability is plummeting, and their employee engagement numbers are plummeting faster than their profitability. And apart from that, their technology belongs in a museum.

When he arrives his boss tells him, 'Your work space isn't quite ready, so let me take you round to where you'll be sitting for now and introduce you to your No. 2.'

'Great. I'd like to meet the other people there too.'

'Why? You'll never need to talk to them.'

'But they will be working for me.'

'But... well, okay then,' his boss responds with a hint of tetchy frustration in his voice, 'I'll introduce you to your No. 2 and he can introduce you to the others.'

What kind of culture is this? What kind of man is this? Alan wonders. And quickly discovers. He is immediately asked to restructure the whole team and ensure that he 'restructures' a particular person, Keith, out, for reasons unnamed. Alan wonders, 'What am I doing in a place like this? Where's God in this?' It's more like the court of Xerxes with Haman plotting the destruction of Mordecai and all his people (Esther 3), or the satraps of Babylon conspiring against Daniel (Daniel 3:3–16).

I wonder how you would respond in a situation like that.

In the event, Alan tells his younger boss that he won't be restructuring the team quite yet – how can he do that before he knows what people can do?

About a month into his new role he offers everyone in his team half an hour of his time. They can, he tells them, talk about anything – career, family, hopes, ambition, God. Most of them, he discovers, aren't happy in their work – the leadership is poor, the politicking rife, the appreciation non-existent, genuine interest or care for people absent... Alan's 'half hour' opens the floodgates for genuine communication: 'People told me all kinds of things. One man, John, was an outstanding performer, on the cusp of being given more responsibility. He told me that he'd been divorced, that his daughter lived with his ex-wife, was suffering from a severe case of anorexia nervosa, and wanted to live with him... He was in tears in my office. Actually over 50% of the people told me really quite personal things. None of them had ever had a conversation like that with a manager.'

Alan, it turns out, has done this with every team he's led. He really cares about his people. I can see it in the frustration and outrage and compassion in his eyes. He begins to tell me about another colleague in personal difficulty... and then pauses, 'Maybe that's why I am there'.

Maybe?

And then he tells me about Keith, the man his boss wanted to 'restructure' out. 'I knew Keith had applied for my job and hadn't got it. He'd also applied for my boss' job and hadn't got that either. He told me that he's been divorced. He'd had a very tough year. He was in tears. I could see he was a man of substance, so I told him that we would look at why he hadn't go those two jobs and figure out how he could work towards the next promotion. Keith was flabbergasted.'

Alan also discovered that Keith was the only person in his sub-team who was client-facing. He had all the relationships. If Keith was 'restructured' out, he'd go to another bank and take his clients with him, at a potential future loss of £185 million.

I wonder what strikes you about Alan's approach? What biblical connections do you see?

I wonder what you would do if you were Alan in such a situation.

Well, when it came time for Alan to see his boss, Alan told him that unless they wanted to risk losing £185 million to other banks it would be unwise to get rid of Keith. As for John, Alan asked him whether, given the difficult situation with his daughter, he would prefer, if it were possible, to be made redundant. To Alan's surprise, John leapt at the prospect. Then Alan set about the hard and detailed task of seeing if there was a business case for such a move.

29

Interestingly, the organisational structure that emerged turned out to be the optimal solution for the overall business. Good for John, good for the bank. As Alan commented, 'That's usually the case, do right by the employees, and it will be good for all.' When Alan informed John that it would all go through he prefaced it by outlining his own priorities in life: God, family, people, community, work. John was hugely grateful, and as it turned out, his daughter's situation improved dramatically.

A few months later, Alan tells me, 'Last week my team did five deals. Five deals is outstanding by any measure. Outstanding.' And the employee engagement numbers in the team of 45 that directly reports to him are soaring. The HR department can't understand it. Alan tells them, 'I just talk to people.' They still don't understand it.

It's not surprising really. There's an assumption in some companies that caring about your staff is a nice luxury if you can afford it, but not really essential. The only things that really count are professional competencies and drive. Increasingly, research is showing this to be false. Still, as ever, old attitudes die hard. Doing the best thing for a business, or indeed any organisation, ought to include 'doing the loving thing', the thing that humanises, the thing that honours the other person as created in the image of God, the thing that seeks the best for them in the context they're in, tries to understand their talents, their hopes, their situation.

Paul's prayer for the Philippian Christians sums up the approach: 'I pray that your love may abound more and more in knowledge and depth of insight' (Philippians 1:9).

Yes, Alan has formidable international banking knowledge and outstanding problem-solving insight, but they only take you so far. It was Alan's abounding love, his soul-deep, authentic care for his people, his deep desire to know what they were good at and what would help them be their best at this point in their lives, that shaped the knowledge he sought to acquire and the range of insight he brought to the challenges they were facing.

Maybe that's why God has Alan there: to demonstrate that you really can bank on love.

> 'I pray that your love may abound more and more in knowledge and depth of insight.'
> *Philippians 1:9*

Alan's leadership reminds me of the way Boaz leads his team and protects Ruth in Ruth 2. She's a newly arrived foreigner, a widow, and so poor that to feed herself and her mother-in-law she has to glean fallen grains of barley in a stranger's field. Boaz, the wealthy owner, recognising that she's so poor that she might not have anything to eat at lunch, provides for her immediate needs by ensuring she has access to water and by offering her roasted grain. He then proactively provides for her medium-term needs by encouraging her to glean in his fields until the end of the harvest season, and by creatively empowering his workers to leave whole stalks of grain on the ground so she could increase her personal harvest. Furthermore, recognising her vulnerability as a single woman in a corrupt society, he deliberately goes out of his way to protect her from sexual harassment, telling the young men not to touch her and alleviating any fears Ruth might have had by telling her that's what he's done. In addition, he both praises her character and prays for her:

'May the Lord repay you for what you have done. May you be richly rewarded by the Lord, the God of Israel, under whose wings you have come to take refuge.' (Ruth 2:12)

Boaz doesn't have to do any of these things. The only thing that the law requires is that he allows her to glean. But the law was not there to limit love but to inspire it and Boaz responds creatively to the needs of the person in front of him, not only physical but social, inviting her to sit with him and the team at lunchtime. Love abounds.

As it did with Alan. He didn't have to go out of his way to develop a business solution that would also benefit John, but he did it.

These days Alan can see why God has him there. That doesn't mean that his boss' attitude to people has changed. It doesn't mean that the overall culture in the bank has changed, even if the climate in his own team has. And it doesn't mean that he will be there in a year's time. Or that he wants to be there right now. Actually, he doesn't. But it does mean that he's confident that he's in the right place for now, confident that he's not wasting his time, confident that God is at work.

After all, take Alan out of the equation, and Keith gets fired, John gets more work to do at a time when he needs less, half the team leave, that department misses its targets, the young boss gets demoted...

Take you – the salt, the light – out of your frontline, your gym, your bus route... and maybe something good doesn't happen, the light doesn't shine, the salt doesn't do its work...

• • •

What are the challenges in the places you spend time during your week?
How do you imagine Christ sees them?

'Come and hear,
all you who fear God;
let me tell you what he
has done for me'

Psalm 66:16

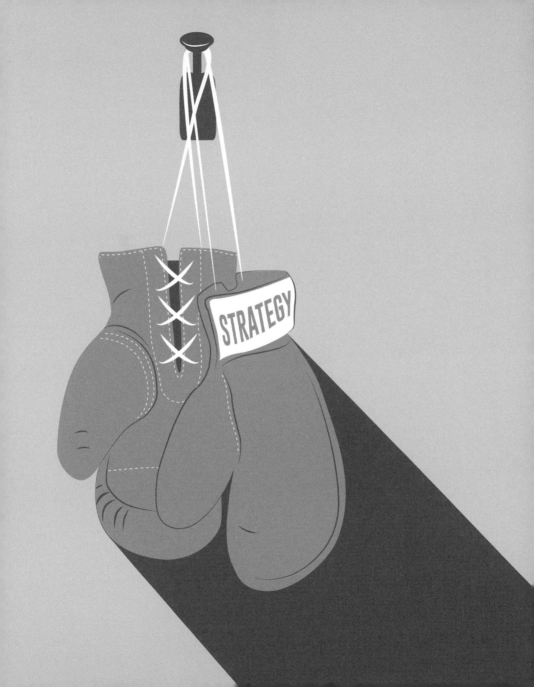

The one about...
the great negotiator

Tomorrow is a big day.

It's the day that Ruth goes in to negotiate her remuneration rates with one of her major clients. It's important that it goes well – it will certainly affect her income for the year and it might well affect whether she gets any income at all from that client.

Ruth is a senior management trainer. She's been doing it for over twenty years for a whole variety of both private and public sector organisations – she trains teams and coaches leaders in a whole range of skills from strategy to conflict resolution to communication to negotiation. Some of the business comes to her directly and some of it comes through the big training companies who outsource work to a list of preferred trainers at rates they negotiate with their clients.

Tomorrow is a big day. And Ruth is praying about it.

Actually, Ruth would be praying even if tomorrow wasn't a particularly special day. She's that kind of person: she prays about her clients, she prays about the content of workshops, she prays about how to deliver the material, she prays for the people who come, and she prays for the people who've left. And when she gets to the training room/auditorium she's been assigned, she accepts the authority that her client has given her over that room. So she prays for it to be a place of peace and safety for her clients, prays for God's presence by his Spirit. So it's no surprise that Ruth is praying about tomorrow. But it is also a big day.

I wonder what you might pray before a meeting to discuss your salary.

Now, as Ruth prays, a curious thing happens. God tells her not to go in to the meeting with a target rate in mind, or even an opening offer to negotiate from. God tells her to give the client total freedom in setting the rate, and to accept whatever they decide.

Ruth is not impressed by the divine strategy.

She demurs. 'Lord,' she says to the King of the Universe, the Lord of time and eternity, the Creator of all things, the one who spoke light and human beings and all their faculties into existence. 'Lord, I'd just like to remind you that I actually teach negotiating skills, and I can assure you that this is not the way to negotiate a deal like this'. Ruth thinks she knows the criteria for a good negotiation, just as the prophet Samuel thought he knew the criteria for selecting the next king from a line-up of Jesse's seven oldest sons: 'When they arrived, Samuel saw Eliab, and thought, "Surely the Lord's anointed stand here before the Lord"'. (1 Samuel 16:6) Except, of course, neither Ruth nor Samuel had all the information.

As it turns out, the King of the Universe is not impressed by Ruth's objection. He does not demur.

I wonder how you would feel if God asked you to do something that seemed to contradict your professional training. I wonder what you would do in Ruth's situation.

Tomorrow arrives.

That morning another senior trainer phones her. He seems pleased. He too has been negotiating his rate with this training company. So Ruth asks him if he got the rate he wanted. 'Oh yes', he replies and mentions a figure. As Ruth is pondering this potentially useful information on what the client is prepared to pay, the Holy Spirit cuts across her thoughts and very clearly reminds her of his strategy. This time she does not demur.

At the appointed time Ruth goes into the client's office, sits down, exchanges greetings. The client looks tense. It's understandable: not many people really like talking about money, and there's usually pressure on the negotiator on three fronts: from the trainers who want to maximise their earnings; from the clients who want to minimise their spend; and from the negotiator's bosses who want to maximise their

I wonder what strikes you about this story so far. What biblical connections do you see?

margin whilst retaining the best trainers and offering competitive value to clients.

Ruth shifts the conversation to the matter in hand and says, 'Before we begin this discussion, may I just say that I will be very happy with whatever rate you choose to give me this year. You're aware of the overall market, you know what clients will pay, and you know what margin you need, so I am happy for you to set whatever rate seems right to you.'

This is not the way money negotiations usually begin.

Immediately, all the tension goes out of the client's face and shoulders. He leans back in his chair and smiles, 'I'm so glad you said that. I was in a very tough negotiation with another senior trainer earlier today. He pushed me very hard for a high rate. And in the end I gave it to him. But I won't be sending any business his way.'

Inwardly Ruth is thankful, not because she's gloating over the other trainer's failure, but because she's realising that God has rescued her. God has tipped her off, given her an instruction based on knowledge she doesn't have. Similar examples abound in the Bible: God tipping off the prophet Elisha whenever Aramean raiding parties set out to ambush the King of Israel (2 Kings 6:9–12); or God giving Samuel information for Saul about who he will meet on his journey home (1 Samuel 10:2–3); or God confirming to David, on the run from King Saul, that, if he stays in Keilah,

the citizens will betray him and his men (1 Samuel 23:10–11). Not surprisingly, God's tip-offs are often accompanied by a blessing. And so it was for Ruth.

The client smiles again. 'And because of your attitude in this negotiation and your track record with us, I am going to make you our trainer of choice for a large project that has just come in.' He then suggested a very acceptable daily rate.

God hasn't just tipped her off, God has given her preferred status.

The client went on, handing Ruth a list of dates, 'And these are the dates. Choose the ones you want.'

God hasn't just tipped her off, God hasn't just given her preferred status, God has blessed her with an abundance of business on the dates and in the locations of her choice.

Three months after Ruth first told me that story, I saw her again at another training event. And I asked her this question. 'Ruth, you teach negotiation skills. So what have you changed about how you teach negotiating after that incident?'

Without missing a beat, she replied, 'I teach people to spend much more time thinking about the other person's context and pressures, to seek to understand how they might be feeling. And I put more emphasis on negotiating in ways that contribute to building the relationship for the longer term.'

God did a miracle for Ruth. And we could pause there and reflect on his omniscience, on his fatherly kindness to Ruth, on his generosity, on his desire to help her know when it's his voice that's speaking, on his desire to build the trust between them, on his desire to build her capacity to trust his direction – even when the stakes are high. And there's more you might add. But God was also trying to teach Ruth about the thing she thought she knew really well: how to negotiate. And so he didn't just provide for her for a year, he enhanced the quality of her

'The man of God sent word to the king of Israel: "Beware of passing that place, because the Arameans are going down there." So the king of Israel checked on the place indicated by the man of God. Time and again Elisha warned the king, so that he was on his guard in such places.

This enraged the king of Aram. He summoned his officers and demanded of them, "Tell me! Which of us is on the side of the king of Israel?"

"None of us, my lord the king," said one of his officers, "but Elisha, the prophet who is in Israel, tells the king of Israel the very words you speak in your bedroom."'
2 Kings 6:9–12

teaching, made it more accurately reflect his character and priorities, made it a greater blessing to those who heard it, a more effective bridge into the deeper conversations with clients that they often seemed to initiate in breaks or at the end of the day...

God, it seems, often has more than one objective in mind when he acts in our lives. We, after all, often have more than one thing we need to learn.

• • •

Is there a situation that you need to pray about, and ask God's wisdom for?

'My mouth will tell of your
righteous deeds, of your
saving acts all day long –
though I know not how to
relate them all.'

Psalm 71:15

The one about...

Little
John

Little John is not. Like his namesake he is big – big for his age, big for any age – the kind of man who looks too big in a suit that's the right size for him. He's 19 and he's just gone up to Uni to study geography. He's also gone up to play rugby. He's keen. At the Freshers' Fair he makes for the Rugby Club stand like a flanker makes for a fly-half with the ball. They're keen too. Ben is rather good, good enough, it soon transpires, to play for the University. Still, he discovers, there is rather more to becoming part of the team than signing up, training at full-throttle, and practising hard.

There's the initiation ceremony.

And the Rugby Club initiation ceremony takes the Freshers' Week tradition of the gargantuan consumption of alcohol to oceanic levels. It's the culture, despite the irony that no professional coach in any sport regards high alcohol intake as a helpful ingredient in developing elite athletic performance. John, for his part, had long before made his own determination before God that alcohol would not form any part of his fitness regime. He knows that being a Christian isn't exactly a fashion statement in contemporary university life and he certainly doesn't want Jesus to be seen as a judgemental killjoy. He also knows that initiation ceremonies are important in building team spirit. And he wants to show that he wants to be part of the team. And it's only one evening. But is this a price he is prepared to pay? Or is there another way?

I wonder what you might do. What biblical connections might you draw on?

Little John prays. Which tells you that he's confident that God will give him wisdom for the situation he's in. It also tells you that he's confident that the King of the Universe is not uninterested in something as mundane as running around a field in pursuit of a ball that doesn't bounce right.

John decides to offer to drink milk instead of alcohol – a pint for every shot of vodka or glass of wine. This is not as wimpy as it sounds. The human body finds it hard to process large amounts of lactose, so drinking large quantities of milk is not only unpleasant but tends to have a similar effect on the contents of one's stomach as large quantities of alcohol.

And this was deemed as sufficiently sacrificial and physically unpleasant to meet the initiation criteria for a sport that requires its participants to undergo a significant amount of physical discomfort.

John's decision is reminiscent of Daniel's as a young Israelite student at Imperial College, Babylon (Daniel 1). Daniel embraced his educational opportunity. He let himself be renamed after a Babylonian god, he studied and mastered their idolatrous literature and he was ready to work for a pagan King.

However, for reasons that scholars have never fully fathomed, he drew the line at the requirement to eat the rich food from the King's table. At the same time, Daniel understood what his immediate supervisor's issue was – it wasn't whether he ate the King's food, it was whether he stays healthy.

So, Daniel suggested a different diet that he thought would still meet his boss' objective, just as Little John suggested a different drink that had the potential to meet the Rugby Club's nausea-inducing objective.

'But Daniel resolved not to defile himself with the royal food and wine, and he asked the chief official for permission not to defile himself in this way. Now God had caused the official to show favour and compassion to Daniel, but the official told Daniel, "I am afraid of my lord the king, who has assigned your food and drink. Why should he see you looking worse than the other young men of your age? The king would then have my head because of you."'
Daniel 1:8–10

FRESH

As it turns out, John became one of
the team's most exuberant socialites,
effervescently sober, confidently
Christian, non-judgementally finding
ways to help others drink less and
offering a way forward to Christians
in other sports teams.

John found a way to be in the
world, but not of it, to contribute
wholeheartedly, without compromise.

MILK

• • •

Is there a situation in your life where you
need God's help to find a creative solution
to a seemingly impossible problem?

'Let the redeemed of the LORD tell their story - those he redeemed from the hand of the foe...'

Psalm 107:2

The one about...
the girl with a schedule in her eyes

Rachel is one of those people who likes to be organised.

Happily for her, she's also one of those people who's rather good at it. Which, at this particular time, is just as well, because it's busy for Rachel. She and her husband and her two children, aged 2 and 4, have just moved house. And they haven't just moved house but city as well. And not just city but church, and not just city and church, but jobs.

For Rachel that's three days working as a creative in a local charity. For her husband it's full-time in a school going through difficulties. And that means he's less around than he wants to be and less around than everyone else wants him to be.

But Rachel is organised, she has her schedule. And if she works her schedule, her schedule works, which is why she rather prefers to keep to it.

And so it comes to pass that on one of those days that she's not working at the charity, she's at the school gate, dropping off her daughter and chatting to another mum who happens to know her mother-in-law... So far, this is all fine because her schedule allows time for incidental chats at the school gate. But then the woman invites herself round to Rachel's house for coffee – there and then.

Invites herself!

There and then!

It's not far to Rachel's house. It's actually just round the corner, but this is not part of Rachel's schedule. Frankly, she's irritated. She's irritated because this is not part of the schedule. She's irritated because she has other things to do in this time slot – errands to run, cleaning to complete. And she's irritated because, despite her formidable communication skills, she's not found the right, warm, affirming, and polite way to say, 'It's really not that convenient today but two weeks on Tuesday would be perfect. At 9.10?'

But she doesn't find the right way to say that, or any way at all for that matter. And so the woman comes round.

How do you tend to respond to inconvenient interruptions?

And Rachel welcomes her in her usual warm way, jauntily concealing her simmering irritation. And then it happens... with the kettle boiling, the chosen mugs popped on the counter, the rectangular tea bags dropped into place, the milk plucked from the fridge... then it hits her.

Maybe the things she had planned to do in this time slot don't actually really have to happen in this time slot. And they don't. She realises that her two days a week away from the charity give her something immensely precious – flexibility. It's a flexibility very few people have in paid work. After all, not many people in paid or volunteer jobs can just saunter off for a long chat with someone at 9.10 on a Tuesday morning. She begins to wonder: what might she do with this gift? Now, this morning, with this woman. And what, in the future, might God want her to do with this gift?

The woman stays for an hour and a half. An hour and a half! It turns out that there's a good reason why she really wanted to talk to someone, and not just anyone, but someone like Rachel, who is not only rather good at being organised but also has a steadiness about her, a kindness, an openness, and a warmth that makes her the kind of person that people instinctively feel they can trust. Happily, Rachel is the kind of person you can trust.

Afterwards Rachel reflects on what happened, on the good that seemed to come out of the conversation for the other woman. And then she begins to realise that God was doing something else that wasn't about the other woman at all, it was about her.

Yes, she has lots to do, but that doesn't mean that it always has to be done at particular times in a particular order. She can move things around, adjust her schedule, take time to talk to a mum who needs to talk, do the errand tomorrow, clean the house in the afternoon, complete next week's schedule after lunch. More deeply, she recognises that for all the benefits of having a schedule, she had made it *her* schedule – she hadn't given it to God. And God, on that morning, had something else on his agenda. As it says in Proverbs, 'Many are the plans in a person's heart, but it is the LORD's purpose that prevails' (Proverbs 19:21). Rachel realises that she had been holding on to her plans too tightly. She hadn't given her plans, her time, her schedule to God. She hadn't relinquished her schedule to God's schedule.

It's not easy to do. It's not easy to discern between interruption and divine interruption, to develop the skill to trust that God might be in the interruption, to ask to see the situation, the person from his point of view. Oh yes, Rachel has learned to trust God for all kinds of things: for work, for finances, for the right home at the right price in the place God wants them to be... big things. Yet somehow it's actually easier to trust God with the big things – they are big, obvious, unavoidable – but to walk through one's day learning to trust God in all its little things, in the planned things and the diversions and the stop signs and the delays, that's something else.

Over the weeks Rachel continues to reflect and realises it is not first and foremost a question of God's authority or his right to interrupt her day and send her off like Jonah to preach to non-believers in Nineveh (Jonah 1:2). No, it isn't primarily about his authority, it's more that she realises that God wants to abide with her in her day, to walk in it with her, to live in it with her, to so be in her that she sees things through his eyes. 'I pray,' Jesus prays the night before his execution, '...that all of them may be one, Father, just as you are in me and I am in you. May they also be in us so that the world may believe that you have sent me' (John 17:20–21).

> 'I pray that all of them may be one, Father, just as you are in me and I am in you. May they also be in us so that the world may believe that you have sent me.'
> *John 17:20–21*

This isn't, she realises, primarily about authority but about relationship. And in this instance it isn't primarily about hearing God's voice, about having ears to hear, but about seeing things differently, about having eyes to see, about learning that the right vantage point to take is the vantage point God takes. Why has God brought this woman to me? What does he want me to bless her with?

Since then, Rachel's been walking around with her eyes wide open. She's been observing how this community of mums works. She's joined the city's mums' group on Facebook. There are lots of them on there – 4000. And they're very open about their struggles, about their brokenness, about husbands who have betrayed them, partners who have left them, children who are sick, pressures at work, pressures without work... And the responses are moving too – full of kindness, compassion, and encouragement.

Rachel's eyes are open now to the behind-the-doors-reality of so many mums' lives, and that's made her eager for God to give her opportunities to share his transforming love – in his time. Whatever her schedule.

• • •

Reflecting back on your day or a recent event, can you see what God might have been doing, or how he might have wanted you to respond?

'I will extol the LORD
with all my heart
In the council of the upright
and in the assembly.'

Psalm 111:1

the man in the tool room

Hugh makes his way across the factory floor, across to the tool room where they make the moulds. There are twelve work benches there, each 10ft by 4ft with a vice on each side.

There are a few small jobs on the benches, bits and bobs, repairs to this and that, but no work on new mouldings, none of the work that pays the bills.

It's been like this for a while; for far, far too long a while. The orders haven't been coming in. Most of the work seems to be going to China and it's getting desperate. And if it carries on this way, the mould-makers won't be staying.

I wonder what you might do if your workplace were facing a crisis.

On this particular day, as Hugh makes his way into the tool room, the mould-makers are sitting around talking, eating lunch. He goes to each workbench, lays hands on it and says, 'Let this bench be full, in Jesus' name'. Twelve benches, twelve prayers.

He does this for six working days in a row.

Almost immediately after that, the managing director receives 72 orders in a single day.

Unprecedented. Never repeated.

Is anything too hard
for our God?

Order No. 72

'Great are the works
of the LORD;
they are pondered by all
who delight in them.'

Psalm 111:2

The one about...
you

Here's some space to record some moment or time when you were aware of God acting in your life. It doesn't have to be spectacular – God's touch is amazing however it comes – just jot down what happened and how you felt.

If that feels difficult, why not tell someone else the story and ask them to write it down, and reflect back to you what they hear?

Here are a few questions that might help to get you, or them, going. Of course, you could also do this in a small group.

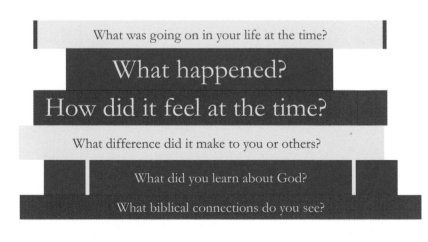

What was going on in your life at the time?

What happened?

How did it feel at the time?

What difference did it make to you or others?

What did you learn about God?

What biblical connections do you see?

Going Further

1. Resources for the journey

If you're interested in material that helps you become more attentive to God and to read your life through the lens of the Bible, here are a few pointers:

Fruitfulness on the Frontline – making a difference where you are:
Brimming with real life stories, Mark Greene's spirit-lifting book offers a liberating framework for fruitfulness to spark our imagination to see how God can work, and has worked, in our everyday lives.

Whole Life, Whole Bible: Antony Billington's compelling walk through the unfolding story of the Bible in 50 reflections shows how our lives are bound up with God's great purposes for the restoration of the universe.

Word for the Week: sign up for LICC's punchy weekly Bible reflection that concisely reflects on a short text and applies it to contemporary life at **licc.org.uk**

2. LICC Prayer Journeys

We've developed a range of 40-day prayer journeys on a variety of themes with very short prayers for the concerns of the day ahead.
Sign up at **licc.org.uk/prayerjourneys**

3. A prayer to try – Examen

Examen is a prayer exercise designed to develop an awareness of God in our daily life that shapes our attitudes and actions. It has five simple steps and takes about 15 minutes to complete.

Examen was developed by Ignatius of Loyola, a soldier by profession. So he understood busyness and pressure, and the need for some tool to help him to be attentive to God both in times of quiet solitude and in the bustle of the day. That's perhaps one of the reasons why, in our pressured times, his prayer exercise, though 500 years old, continues to be used so widely.

This is a simplified version that we've been sharing for around five years.

The Prayer

This is not primarily an intellectual exercise to analyse your day. It's a chance to be still in God's presence and listen out for what he might bring to mind.

1. Being Still

Relax. Allow the tensions of the day to dissipate, and recognise that you are in God's presence.

2. Giving Thanks

Look at your day with gratitude for the gifts God has given you:
a task completed, a relationship deepened, progress made on a project, customers served well.

3. Seeking Inspiration

Ask the Holy Spirit to help you see and understand how his love has been working in you today: how you have used your God-given gifts and abilities, and managed your limitations.

4. Reviewing & Reflecting

Reflect peacefully on what has been happening to you, in you, and through you today. Trust that the Holy Spirit will show you whatever he wants you to see.

You may simply wish to remain silently focused on God during this time of reflection. You might also find a few of the following questions useful in prompting your reflection.

Have you learned anything today about God and his ways,
in the everyday events of living and working?

Where did you meet him in the ups and downs: fears, joys,
misunderstandings, weariness, exhilaration?

Notice your habits and patterns in the day. Which positive ones would you seek
to reinforce? Which negative ones could you lay down with God's help?

Would you do anything differently tomorrow?

5. Reconciling & Preparing

In your reflection you may have noticed moments to celebrate and other moments that caused you sorrow. Thank God for the things that went well, and ask him to show more of his love to others through you. Where your response to God in the day has been inadequate, ask for (and be confident in) his forgiveness, and rejoice at God's deep desire to help you love him and others well.

Finally, look forward to tomorrow. Ask for sensitivity to recognise God's promptings in the day, and courage and wisdom to act upon them. Pray for an open heart and open hands to minister to those around you as opportunities arise. If you already know that you will be facing challenging situations, ask for wisdom and a right heart attitude. Invite God to be with you in each situation.

About The London Institute for Contemporary Christianity

What difference does following Jesus make to our ordinary daily lives, to the things we normally do, in the places we normally spend time, with the people we usually meet? How can we live fruitfully and faithfully, sharing and showing the love and wisdom and ways of Christ right where we are?

Back in 1982, LICC was founded to answer that question by one of the greatest and most influential Bible teachers and Christian leaders of the 20th century – John Stott. He and his co-founders wanted to change the story of the church in the UK and indeed globally, change it to a story of God's people envisioned, empowered, encouraged, and sent into their everyday contexts confident in him, in the necessity and beauty of his plan of salvation, and in his call to join in his transformative purposes for every nook of his world.

Today the team at LICC works with Christians and leaders from across the denominations seeking to help Christians make a difference for Christ out on their daily frontlines, to help church leaders help them, and to help theological educators train church leaders to make fruitful whole-life disciples for the whole of life – for the blessing of our nation and the salvation of many.

Join us. To find out more, go to **licc.org.uk**

licc.
The London Institute for
Contemporary Christianity